The Ea[illegible]ory

Daily Pra[illegible] Creation

Steven Shakespeare

First published in 2019 by the Canterbury Press Norwich
Editorial office
3rd Floor, Invicta House
108–114 Golden Lane
London EC1Y 0TG, UK
www.canterburypress.co.uk

Canterbury Press is an imprint of Hymns Ancient & Modern Ltd
(a registered charity)

British Library Cataloguing in Publication data

A catalogue record for this book is available
from the British Library

978 1-78622-228-2

Typeset by Manila Typesetting Company
Printed and bound in Great Britain by
CPI Group (UK) Ltd

FROM KATHRYN

Contents

Acknowledgements v
Introduction vii

Part One Praying with the Seasons 1

The Path of Shadows 3
The Growing Light 15
The Seed of Promise 26
The Fire of Life 38
The Greatest Light 50
The Gift of First Fruits 61
The Time of Gathering 74
The Call of Memory 87

Part Two Praying with the Elements 101

Praying with Air 105
Praying with Fire 110
Praying with Water 115
Praying with Earth 120

Appendix: Canticles 125

This book is dedicated to the FISH children's group at St Bride's, Liverpool, and to my co-leaders: Sandra, Emma and Sally, with thanks for the wisdom and laughter

Acknowledgements

I would like to thank Sally, Ben and Jake for their love and support. I am also grateful to friends Mike Finn, Gary Anderson and Niamh Malone in particular who were never short of theological insights and bad puns. Conversations with Mark Waters, Eleanor Rees and other poets and seekers have been really enriching. And, despite all the market pressures and compromises of modern higher education, the Department of Theology, Philosophy and Religious Studies at Liverpool Hope University has always been a fabulous place to share ideas and interests with people passionate about wisdom and spirituality.

A special thanks to the community at St Bride's, Liverpool, not least for kindly welcoming my fumbling experiments in writing prayer and liturgy. The church's FISH children's group and leaders have helped to keep me grounded and inspired, and it is to them that this collection is dedicated.

Introduction

Some time ago, I wrote a book called *Prayers for an Inclusive Church.*[1] I followed the three-year lectionary used by many churches, and created a prayer for each Sunday in that cycle. I also wrote a number of seasonal sets of prayers for the celebration of the Eucharist. My aim was to write in a way that reflected an inclusive, but biblically rooted spirituality. Each of the Sunday prayers was related to the Gospel reading set for that day. I hoped this meant they would be usable in a variety of contexts, wherever those Gospel themes were in focus. However, the book was set out mainly as a resource for worship leaders who were following the lectionary pattern. Over the years, it has been encouraging to hear from those who found the book helpful, and to learn of examples of it being used in churches across the world (including the Anglican Church in Canada, where moves are being made to incorporate some of those prayers into authorized usage).

---

1 *Prayers for an Inclusive Church*, Norwich: Canterbury Press, 2008.

The present book is not intended to be a continuation to *Prayers for an Inclusive Church.* I have deliberately taken a very different approach, and a few words about this may help orient the reader.

I have been inspired by three main aims: to create something appropriate for daily prayer; to deepen my exploration of inclusivity; and, especially, to embed the prayers more deeply in the veneration of creation. I will say a little more about each of these.

Daily Prayer

Following the Eucharistic/Sunday focus of my previous book, I wanted to fashion a collection that would work for regular daily prayer, whether for individuals or for small groups. Of course, the prayers or sets of responses from this book can be used in bigger gatherings, including Sunday worship, but that has not been my guiding motivation.

Many people are looking for ways to integrate spirituality and daily life. The popularity of forms of daily prayer and meditation practices, rules of life, retreats and more bear witness to this. Spirituality is not something to be compartmentalized, but is the atmosphere of a life.

This collection is offered as a resource to aid people in this quest. Part One, 'Praying with the Seasons', offers a set of rites for daily use. Part Two, 'Praying with the Elements', contains four rites for occasional use.

I have tried to offer words that might resonate and inspire, but to keep everything in a very simple structure. Some 'daily offices' abound in complexities and options; and while these work for some, for many they are cumbersome, wordy and difficult to negotiate. They can demand a good head for rules and a large selection of bookmarks! I have erred on the side of simplicity, offering scope for users to expand on the material here through the readings, music and symbolic practices they might choose. If used regularly, this has the advantage that the prayers can easily become familiar. In this way, the prayers can become less about conscious focus on the words, and more of a 'second nature', a rhythm that works at a deeper level.

Deepening Inclusivity

The second aim is clearly to be true to some of the principles of inclusive worship and language I tried to adhere to in my previous book, but also to build on them. At the time of writing *Prayers for an Inclusive Church*, I was convinced that inclusivity in liturgical writing is more than just using gender neutral language. It is also about structures of power and privilege, and how these are named and shaken by the practices and forms of a worshipping community. This insurrectionary power of a living theology has borne fruit again and again in our recent history, including struggles against white supremacy and for the blackness of Christ, as well as radical challenges to patriarchy and the whole raft of ways in which the white, able-bodied male becomes the 'norm' for humanity (and so for God, in whose image humanity is made). A book of prayers cannot substitute for that praxis, but my aim has been to write in ways that convey the *actively* subversive and transformational potentials of the gospel, while making space for the messiness of actual human experience. In this – as a white, able-bodied male – I am always only a learner (from figures such as James Cone, Marcella Althaus-Reid, Rosemary Radford Ruether, Carter Heywood, J. Kameron Carter, Lisa Isherwood, Catherine Keller, Chung Hyun Kyung, Kwok Pui-lan, Delores Williams and Nancy Eiesland). We are differently bodied and voiced, and that is a richness, not a threat, nor something to be controlled by the imposition of social norms and violence. However, beyond the mere affirmation of 'difference', there needs to be attention paid to the differences that *matter*, the differences that challenge power and liberate from systematic violence and marginalization. If inclusion is limited to bland tolerance, it easily colludes with the status quo.

That said, I wanted to maintain a link with traditional forms, including the language of addressing God or Jesus as 'Lord'. The motivation was to suggest that if Jesus is Lord, *no one else is*: no earthly power of domination can claim the place of the sacred. Instead, Jesus offers a 'lordship' of servanthood, empowerment, and the disabling of social status. This lordship was diametrically opposed to imperial power and challenged the empire of his time, which classed him as a criminal traitor.

Despite this, the language of Lordship, with its connotations of masculine power over others, still jarred for some. While there are creative potentials in repurposing such language to subvert its customary meanings, there is also a place for ways of praying that simply do away with it. Empires have not gone away in our time – far from it – but they are known and named differently. In a new context, calling Jesus 'Lord' may have as much to do with conservative reaction and romanticism about hierarchy as it does with radical hospitality and inclusion.

I have, then, experimented a bit more with my use of language, thinking more broadly about the dimensions of inclusion. Hopefully, I have avoided being didactic, or just trying to name-check every area of inclusion. This would be a futile, tokenistic exercise which would miss the way in which prayer finds its clarity and critical prophetic edge precisely by inhabiting more deeply the dimensions of affect, intuition, poetry and unknowing. Prayer has always been for me more of an attunement to an environment of radical acceptance than a shopping list of demands or a sermon in disguise. If I fall short of this at times, that at least is the aim.

This leads on to the third aim I have set for this collection, which is to engage more deeply in these habits of prayer through a creation-centred spirituality.

Praying with Creation

We are clearly living in a time when the impact of human activity on the earth has reached crisis point.

Climate change, the massive loss of biodiversity, the ongoing issues of sea, fresh water and air pollution, the industrial levels of cruelty visited upon animals reared for food or used in experiments – all of this speaks of a relationship to our ecology that is badly out of joint. I am convinced this is a problem both of public policy and, broadly speaking, of an embodied *spirituality*. By this I mean our sense of ourselves as related to the ultimate significance, presence and value of things, embodied in the way we give (or fail to give) attention, understanding, compassion and delight to the webs of created life of which we are part.

It is this motivation that has inspired a different approach to the seasonal pattern of the year which organizes Part One, 'Praying with the Seasons'. Rather than follow the standard Christian liturgical year, I have opted instead to divide the year into eight roughly equal sections. These sections are tied to the key points of the solar calendar: the spring and autumn equinoxes and the summer and winter solstices. In between these turning points are four other significant dates, often known as 'fire festivals' in contemporary pagan spirituality, because of the use of bonfires and other flames in marking them.

The mention of pagan spirituality indicates that my use of this pattern is hardly something original. It has been adopted by those seeking a way of reflecting the rhythm or flow of the seasons. In this cycle, nature and spirit are not seen as opposed, but resonate with each other's depths.

What may be more unusual is the employment of such a pattern for a Christian book of prayers, and this is worth a word or two of explanation. I adopt it both as a corrective and as a stimulus. It is a corrective, because we often falsely juxtapose Christian and pre-Christian spiritualities. In fact, the Christian year itself reflects (or commandeers!) many pre-Christian celebrations. And there is a strong tradition of Christian prayer and witness that is rooted in the being, the 'suchness' of creation. It is the prayer of Celtic saints on exposed islands as much as desert mothers and fathers in the scorching wilderness. This was not an easy sentimentalism about 'nature'. In the strangeness and otherness of creation, they sought an abandonment of false living, and exposure to the often harrowing nearness and risk of unconditioned love. Rediscovering the 'thin places' where the divine is present is a reminder that locating God in some faraway heaven is ironically a way of *belittling* God: locating and defining 'him' according to our assumptions about power and divinity. What is more, the idea that Christianity tends towards the unearthly, or that we should see ourselves as detached rulers and consumers of nature, is a false spirituality that has surely contributed to our contemporary ecological and social disasters.

My claim is that adopting an alternative way of inhabiting the year can therefore also be a stimulus to imagine the cadence of Christian life and prayer differently, to embody spirituality differently. The old stereotype that pre-Christian faiths were cyclical while Christianity is linear (moving from past to future) is hard to sustain. The calendars of the Hebrew Scriptures and of the Christian Church clearly operate with cyclical patterns, and are none the worse for that. They respond to the particular rhythms of creation and food production, in ways that can expose us anew to something other than our 'always on' social imperatives of consumerism and season-less food. Perhaps they may also make us aware of the destructive costs of our alienation from how the earth is tended and how food is produced. These hidden costs are heavy, both for humans and for the creatures and ecosystems we exploit for our own unsustainable advantage.

Since the standard church calendars often track the solar one, my approach is not totally detached from that tradition, but can cast new light on old festivals and seasons. I do not assume that pagan and Christian traditions are essentially saying the same thing, only that their insights can speak to one another fruitfully. In this way, Christians might re-evaluate our ways of praying with creation, and those who follow other spiritual traditions might find new dimensions to Christianity.

This rootedness in the seasons does, however, place a limitation on the geographical reach this book can have. It is undoubtedly more suited to the northern hemisphere, where, for example, the winter solstice and Christmas nearly coincide. Playing with these connections has allowed me to give particular shape to the prayers, while limiting their universality. But that is to be expected: inclusion is never about bland uniformity, and other ways and words will be found and made in other contexts. Some attention to the specificity of place and climate is part and parcel of reconnecting to our living ecosystems.

As mentioned, I offer a little flexibility outside of this daily pattern by also including four simple rites focused on 'Praying with the Elements', which you will find in Part Two of the book. In ancient thought, it was speculated that the ultimate constituents of the world were fourfold: air, fire, water and earth. While science has long since left this system behind as analysis, as myth and symbol its resonances remain strong. The four elements can themselves be associated with the different seasons and stages of life. They also can be connected with spiritual qualities: air with thought and inspiration; fire with passion and desire; water with intuition and purification; earth with stability and rootedness.

In creating these four additional rites, I have incorporated some of these connections, as well as building upon the rich vein of scriptural engagements with the elements. They are offered for people to use as and when appropriate, when the daily rites are perhaps not striking the right chord. They may be helpful when a particular mood, stage of life or experience is dominant; or perhaps inserted into the course of the year at special moments of intensity.

Using the Prayers

In Part One, although I have composed my own titles for the seasons, they map on to the eightfold division used elsewhere. Including the approximate times of the festivals, and my suggestions for when each seasonal set of prayers should be used, the pattern looks like this:

Prayer section	Seasonal festival	Christian calendar	Suggested timing
The Path of Shadows	Winter solstice 21/22 December	Advent and Christmas	Advent Sunday – Epiphany
The Growing Light	First festival of the new spring (Imbolc) 1 February	Epiphany and Candlemas	Epiphany – beginning of Lent
The Seed of Promise	Spring equinox Around 20/21 March	Lent	Lent
The Fire of Life	Festival of the height of spring (Beltane) 1 May	Easter and Pentecost	Easter Sunday – Pentecost
The Greatest Light	Summer solstice 20/21 June	No specific association – ordinary time	Pentecost – end of July
The Gift of First Fruits	Festival of first fruits (Lughnasadh) 1 August	Lammas ('loaf mass') Day/ ordinary time	August – early September
The Time of Gathering	Autumn equinox Around 22/23 September	Harvest/ ordinary time	Early September – late October
The Call of Memory	Festival of the ancestors (Samhain) 1 November	All Souls, All Saints	Late October – Advent Sunday

There is some flexibility built into this, and users are free to decide just when to make the transition from one season to another. Some may simply wish to dip into the collection from time to time or use it as a resource to help create other celebrations.

The way this eightfold division tracks the seasons is especially important in a temperate climate. The solstices mark the end points of the ebb and flow of the sun's strength; the equinoxes mark the balance between light and dark. Each one is a transition point, a move into a different season of growth or retreat, life or death. They can help us to connect with the wider natural processes around us – so often kept at a distance by artificial lighting and food production – and also cause us to reflect on our own personal and communal cycles of new birth and letting go.

The fire festivals offer additional staging posts in this journey. They originally held importance as agricultural turning points: of sowing, fruition and early and late harvests. Imbolc is associated with the first stirrings of spring, with new birth, healing and purification; Beltane with fire, fertility, ecstasy and fulfilment; Lughnasadh with the start of harvest, gatherings and games; and Samhain with memory and integration. The latter was also a time when the spiritual word and this world were closely intertwined, when social norms could be suspended, the spirits of the dead were present and ancestors were revered. It is no accident that the Christian festivals of All Hallows, All Saints and All Souls overlap with it.

The Christian calendar connects with this eightfold pattern in many other ways, as the table above suggests.

Again, I am not claiming that their meanings – which in any case are multiple – are just the same, only that there is a rich web of connections and differences that help us to feel with new senses the meaning of Christian rites and the spirit of creation.

We should be past the stage where Christians indulge in lazy generalizations about other faith traditions, including the diversity of pagan and neo-pagan paths. As with any encounter, there will always be room for critique, but moments of openness and empathy are vital to any meeting with otherness. In practice the Christian Church has combined hostility to these traditions with a readiness to 'baptize' their sacred places and times, so there has always been a hidden dialogue taking place, however skewed by power and coercion. Perhaps now is the time for that dialogue to come into the light, to be carried out with humility and grace.

There is, of course, the danger that I am repeating the mistakes of the past by co-opting traditions into the Christian fold. I hope this is not the case. In drawing inspiration from these spiritual cycles, I claim no ownership of them in any way, no sense that they can only be fulfilled or receive their truth in a Christian context.

You may wish to explore these associations further; or simply leave them be and use the prayers as they are offered. The choice is yours, but I hope that these words and rhythms help to connect you to the unconditioned and incarnate grace of God.

In addition to this annual cycle, simple headings structure the day and each individual set of prayers. The day is divided into sets of prayers for Awakening, Pausing, Recalling and Letting Go. These correspond to prayer for the morning, the midst of the day, evening and night respectively. Within each of these occasions for prayer, I use the same structure: Opening, Attending, Offering and Blessing. These patterns clearly draw on the existing dynamics of liturgy – I am not reinventing the wheel! I hope simply to have offered a clear and simple way of acknowledging and working with the structure of each day and each moment, as a dynamic of openness and return. These cycles nest within each other: the pattern of the year echoes in that of each day and each moment of prayer.

I also include some optional canticles, psalm-like prayers inspired by Scripture that can be used to complement the seasonal patterns. These can be found in the Appendix, with a little further explanation. I have not incorporated them into the main body of the prayers, as some users may prefer fewer words and more silence.

As indicated above, Part Two, 'Praying with the Elements', is intended to complement this daily structure. These rites can be used on occasions where a particular focus on the qualities of that element is helpful. They include their own canticles (which can be replaced by others if required).

Bold text is used to indicate words that may be said by everyone, where the prayers are used in a group setting. It is often helpful to have some kind of call and response structure to communal prayer, to create a rhythmic dialogue between the participants. However, these communal passages are only suggestions, and groups may of course decide to use the texts differently.

Final Thought: The Nature of Prayer

In *Prayers for an Inclusive Church*, I tried to explain a little of my own understanding of prayer. I will not repeat that here, other than to reaffirm my conviction that part of praying is unlearning some of the crude and unhelpful notions of prayer that emphasize submission to God's predetermined plan, alongside a frankly incredible conviction that God rearranges the universe to satisfy our individual desires (while seemingly ignoring vast swathes of suffering humanity and creatures).

To end on a more positive note, I wanted to mention how I have been significantly formed by traditions of mystical prayer. The term 'mysticism' is endlessly debated; what I have in mind is an unknowing, which suspends conventional identities as it seeks and finds itself enfolded by the undefinable and unnameable God. This God is not a cosmic dictator, or a human monarch with an ego that needs to be flattered. Rather, God is the unconditional ground and being of reality.

This might make it sound as if mystical prayer were an escape from the world into some sort of emptiness. But the emptiness it seeks is one of letting go of the ego and the false self, and becoming one with all things as an expression of God's infinite reality. It is a deeply embodied prayer, in which human beings are no longer little emperors controlling creation; but we are radically opened to the creative reality and inner being of all things. For Meister Eckhart, or Nicholas of Cusa, there is a radical equality at the heart of prayer: of creature with creature and creature with God. So the unlearning of false notions of God goes hand in hand with a deepening spiritual connection with all that is. As Eckhart puts it: 'So therefore let us pray to God that we may be free of "God," and that we may apprehend and rejoice in that everlasting truth in which the highest angel and the fly and the soul are equal – there where I was established, where I wanted what I was and was what I wanted.'[2] Or, in Cusa's words: 'For who could understand infinite unity, which infinitely precedes all opposition, where all things are enfolded, without composition, in simplicity of unity; where there is neither other nor different; where a human does not differ from a lion and sky does not differ from earth?'[3]

This 'indifference' is not a boring sameness, but a glorious, infinite divinity manifest in and through all difference, in every face and body. Here, it makes no sense to talk of God 'over against' creation; for God is the heartbeat of creativity in all things. Here, prayer becomes truly inclusive, as a deep intuition of the end of all hierarchy, and the liberating inclusion of each one of us into the divine being.

---

2 Meister Eckhart, *The Essential Sermons, Commentaries, Treatises, and Defense*, New York: Paulist Press, 1981, p. 169.

3 Nicholas of Cusa, 'On Learned Ignorance', in *Selected Spiritual Writings*, trans. H. Lawrence Bond, New York: Paulist Press, 1997, p. 122.

PART ONE

Praying with the Seasons

The Path of Shadows

Suggested timing: Advent Sunday – Epiphany

Awakening: Prayer for the day's dawning

OPENING

The morning star rises
in the cold air.
It beckons us,
lifting the soul.

The sun's fingers stretch
through fields and streets.
It reaches us,
kindling the heart.

The sleeping earth stirs,
pulsing with life.
It grounds us,
cradling our roots.

The mist descends
in sparkling dew.
It washes us,
cleansing our awareness.

Silence is kept

We are grateful for this air, this fire, this earth,
this water;
for the elements that make up our world,
our diverse bodies, our souls and our dreams.
May Christ the morning star
reveal the light in all things,
in the wonderful strangeness
of all that we are.

ATTENDING

This is not the time
to think that all is right with the world.
This is not the time
to accept prejudice and poverty.

This is the time
to face the truth of our past,
the shadows of the present,
the promise of what is not yet.

We pray for the mind of Christ:
attentive love,
deep compassion
and a fierce longing that all might have fullness of life.
Amen.

One or more readings or pieces of music may be heard, followed by a time of silence.

An appropriate canticle may be used (see Appendix).

OFFERING

We offer ourselves,
our light and our shadows,
to the sacred circle of love.

Where certainties condemn
and the whiteness of hate
builds temples to itself:
We offer ourselves,
our light and our shadows,
to the sacred circle of love.

Personal prayers for oneself, others and the world may be offered.

Divine mother, divine father:
to be in you is to be in heaven.
May we hear the wonder that echoes in your name.
May we accept no rule but the rule of love.
May we never tolerate the evil of hunger.

May the hurts we cause be forgiven
and the hurts we receive be healed.
May we remember that we are fragile
and cherish the life we share with all.
For all love, and life and power
is the gift of the Spirit.
Amen.

BLESSING

May we tread lightly on the sleeping earth;
may we be cleansed by the shining air;
and may the blessing of the living God,
the God of shadow, seed and silence,
form our hearts and guide our steps.
Amen.

Pausing: Prayer for the day's journey

OPENING

Step aside: let the day breathe.
Look within: let your heart be still.
Listen well: hear the still, small voice,
calling you back to what God has made you to be.

In the middle of all that life offers us
in the eye of all the storms,
we thank you for the gift of this moment,
for the grace of this presence.

ATTENDING

May the word echo
in the chamber of the heart.
May the spirit breathe
in the song of creation.

Give us grace
to feel the brief touch of winter light,
to sense the rhythms of the deep earth,
to know your stillness
at the heart of all things.
Amen.

One or more readings or pieces of music may be heard,
or silence kept.

OFFERING

We offer this moment of stillness
in the stream of time.

To the nurturing root of all life,
we offer all that has been and is to come.

Personal prayers for oneself, others and the world may be offered.

BLESSING

Go with us, Spirit of winter,
across ground hard with cold.
Be the warmth of our heart and hearth,
nurturing new birth.
Amen.

Recalling: Prayer for the lengthening shadows

OPENING

The light dwindles
into the darkness of winter.
It seems so fragile;
but the dark gathers it,
keeps it safe,
helps it to shine.

The life dwindles
into the darkness of earth.
It seems to be lost;
but the dark treasures it,
keeps it rooted,
helps it to rebirth.

The divine dwindles
into the darkness of the womb.
It seems impossible;
but the dark nurtures it,
and the Christ is born
in each of us.

Silence is kept

When the dark threatens us,
when the light dazzles us,
when life overwhelms us,
we remember God is with us
in the gentleness of the dark,
the inspiration of the light
and the courage to be who we are.

God is with us in the gentleness of the dark

ATTENDING

Christ, you travelled with your friends as evening fell,
sharing stories, enflaming hearts.

Turn aside with us and soften the armour
that lies anxious and heavy around our spirit.
We hear you now:
'Do not be afraid. All will be well.'

One or more readings or pieces of music may be heard, followed by a time of silence.

An appropriate canticle may be used (see Appendix).

OFFERING

We hold in your presence
the gifts and wounds of the day.
We thank you for the ways we have grown,
however slow and hidden that growth might be.

In the harvest of this winter evening,
give us a love that nurtures seeds yet to be born.
We offer you the promises born today
and the hopes and fears we carry into the dark.

Personal prayers for oneself, others and the world may be offered.

Divine mother, divine father:
to be in you is to be in heaven.
May we hear the wonder that echoes in your name.

May we accept no rule but the rule of love.
May we never tolerate the evil of hunger.
May the hurts we cause be forgiven
and the hurts we receive be healed.
May we remember that we are fragile
and cherish the life we share with all.
For all love, and life and power
is the gift of the Spirit.
Amen.

BLESSING

This is a time of gifts:
the gift of creation, abundance of life;
the gift of our deepest ground, bearing the divine within us;
the gift of connection, the Spirit of community.
May these gifts be a blessing to us and to all
and may the divine child
show us the way to wisdom and truth.
Amen.

Letting Go: Prayer for the encompassing dark

OPENING

Under the wings of the Spirit,
the Spirit of the shining dark:
let there be rest.

The flame dies down,
the winter moon rises:
let there be rest.

In the ending of the day,
in the time of letting go:
let there be rest.

ATTENDING

The night comes,
easing our anxious grasp,
opening us to untold truth,
dreaming beyond words.
Let us receive the gifts of this night.

One or more readings or pieces of music may be heard, or silence kept.

OFFERING

At the time of greatest darkness
is a surrender of control.

At the time of smallest light
is a life that waits unseen.

Help us let go of what needs to pass.
Help us receive what waits to be born.

Personal prayers for oneself, others and the world may be offered.

Keep us, holy Spirit of air,
under the shadow of your wings.
Keep us, holy Spirit of earth,
in the darkening of your trees.
Keep us, holy Spirit of water,
in the stillness of your depths.
Keep us, holy Spirit of fire,
in the embers of your heart.

Shadow of your wings

Father, I love your spirit of air.

BLESSING

May the God of this night
protect us, surround us, watch us.
May the God of this night
renew us, deepen us, dream us.
May the God of this night
wait with us for the coming dawn.
Amen.

The Growing Light

Suggested timing: Epiphany – beginning of Lent

Awakening: Prayer for the day's dawning

OPENING

We awaken to the quickening of the day
to the first shoots of the greening world.

We greet the rising God
She who comes with the promise of life.

We taste and see her dawning glory
a light of hope, tender and strong.

Silence is kept

The God who dances with the dawn.

Let us drink from her wells
the God who dances with the dawn.

Let us nurture her gifts
the Spirit of new beginnings.

ATTENDING

The sleeping seed needs the yielding soil,
the slow strength of patient time.

May we be open to word and light
and the soft persistence of growing things.

One or more readings or pieces of music may be heard, followed by a time of silence.

An appropriate canticle may be used (see Appendix).

OFFERING

We are connected with all things.
May the weave between us
make strong our fragile hearts.

We pray for all who bear life
within themselves,
within their community,
within the wider world,
even when all seems barren and hard.

Personal prayers for oneself, others and the world may be offered.

Divine mother, divine father:
to be in you is to be in heaven.
May we hear the wonder that echoes in your name.
May we accept no rule but the rule of love.
May we never tolerate the evil of hunger.
May the hurts we cause be forgiven
and the hurts we receive be healed.
May we remember that we are fragile
and cherish the life we share with all.
For all love, and life and power
is the gift of the Spirit.
Amen.

we are fragile

BLESSING

She who was, and is and is to come,
carry us into this day:
sustained by her life-giving waters,
encouraged by her fruitful love,
inspired by the light she kindles.
Amen.

Pausing: Prayer for the day's journey

OPENING

The miracle has begun
in the stirring of life.

Winter's cold heart
thaws in spring light.

The water runs
the earth breathes.

We pause to notice.
We are present.

ATTENDING

Midway in the stream of life
we turn aside.
We listen for the word of Christ
whispering through rock and stream and city street,
in places of work and waiting,
in times of wandering and longing.

Wherever we are,
whoever we are,
this word is for us.

One or more readings or pieces of music may be heard, or silence kept.

OFFERING

We look for the places where new life might appear;
may we help it come to birth.
We look for the times when hurts might be healed;
may we offer compassion.

As we move through our day
may we give and receive blessings,
strange in our imperfect hands.
Let our actions flow from a heart of loving insight.

Personal prayers for oneself, others and the world may be offered.

BLESSING

**Life is rising
in the womb of the earth.
May it enfold us,
sustain us
and inspire us.
Amen.**

Recalling: Prayer for the lengthening shadows

OPENING

The gentling light recedes.
The growing seed rests.
We breathe in the Spirit.

The candle gathers the evening light,
draws us inward to stay a while.
Christ is among us, greeting and sharing.

At the lengthening of the shadows
we rest, assured
that all is being made and remade,
that the glory of life is undimmed,
that no power on earth,
no cruelty or indifference,
can tell the meaning of love
or still its heart.

The gift is being given,
the grace flows on;
we greet it, one in the Maker.

ATTENDING

As evening fell,
the story tells,
Jacob wrestled with God until dawn
and found both wound and blessing.

We are ready now
with the world on our heart,
with our fears for what has not yet grown,
our hurts for what has been lost.

We are ready now
for the wildness of life,
for the childhood of our heart,
still so small and hidden,
to be revealed to us and in us and through us.

We are ready now
imperfect as we are,
to find, within the wounds of time,
the blessing of a limping God,
who never leaves us to dance alone.

One or more readings or pieces of music may be heard, followed by a time of silence.

An appropriate canticle may be used (see Appendix).

OFFERING

As evening draws on
we commend into God's hand and heart
all whose day has been long and hard,
all who are nursing fresh scars
and fragile hopes.

May our prayers find their way
to the circle of the Spirit
and clear the path
to the first glimmer of Spring.

Personal prayers for oneself, others and the world may be offered.

**Divine mother, divine father:
to be in you is to be in heaven.
May we hear the wonder that echoes in your name.
May we accept no rule but the rule of love.
May we never tolerate the evil of hunger.
May the hurts we cause be forgiven
and the hurts we receive be healed.
May we remember that we are fragile
and cherish the life we share with all.
For all love, and life and power
is the gift of the Spirit.
Amen.**

BLESSING

May She bless us.
May She enfold us.
May She guide us.
May the Spirit of new growth
sing with our spirit,
midwife our hopes
and forge our courage.
Amen.

Letting Go: Prayer for the encompassing dark

OPENING

Under the wings of the Spirit,
the Spirit of the shining dark:
let there be rest.

The flame dies down,
the new year's moon is born:
let there be rest.

In the ending of the day,
in the time of letting go:
let there be rest.

ATTENDING

The light is no more
yet all creation speaks:
soft, in the water's flow;
sharp, in the owl's eye;
restless, in the bat's flight.

The light is no more
yet the human spirit speaks:
longing for connection;
tender in care;
foolish and hopeful in desire.

In the darkness
you reach to us,
through all and in all.
Let us hear your voice
and know your gentle love.

One or more readings or pieces of music may be heard, or silence kept.

OFFERING

In Christ all is born anew
within the womb of eternity.
May love be the seed of this new life,
shared with all.

With thanks for the day's gifts
and hope for the dawning light
we give ourselves into your hands.

Personal prayers for oneself, others and the world may be offered.

Keep us, holy Spirit of air,
under the shadow of your wings.
Keep us, holy Spirit of earth,
in the darkening of your trees.
Keep us, holy Spirit of water,
in the stillness of your depths.
Keep us, holy Spirit of fire,
in the embers of your heart.

BLESSING

May your blessing follow us
into the peace of sleep
and the miracle of dreaming.
May your blessing quicken
the life that stirs within us.
Amen.

The Seed of Promise

Suggested timing: Lent

Awakening: Prayer for the day's dawning

OPENING

The seed sheds its husk
and the day emerges,
blinking in the spring light.

As we cast off the shadows
may our spirit rise with the rising sun,
alive and awake in the glowing air.

We give thanks for the gift of this,
all of this,
all of you:
so present, so near.
In the chaos and buzz of life we find you:
a stillness, gentle and immense.

As we give thanks for the day
may our prayers rise like birds from the mist
finding their path to the clear heights.

ATTENDING

In desert places
you come to us
sowing a seed of promise.

Give us grace
to know ourselves more deeply,
to strip away false images,
seeing the world anew.

Help us to listen now
to the unheard stories
and victim voices,
the words of God for our time.

One or more readings or pieces of music may be heard, followed by a time of silence.

An appropriate canticle may be used (see Appendix).

OFFERING

We remember those forced from home
and made to bear the hatred of others.

We remember those neglected and lost
and made to bear the indifference of others.

We remember those haunted by trauma
and made to bear the cruelty of others.

We pray with all on hard roads
and thankless tasks.
We pray to hear those
disabled by the powers of the world.
Bind us in heart and deed
to be companions in all things.

Personal prayers for oneself, others and the world may be offered.

Divine mother, divine father:
to be in you is to be in heaven.
May we hear the wonder that echoes in your name.
May we accept no rule but the rule of love.
May we never tolerate the evil of hunger.
May the hurts we cause be forgiven
and the hurts we receive be healed.
May we remember that we are fragile
and cherish the life we share with all.
For all love, and life and power
is the gift of the Spirit.
Amen.

BLESSING

May the divine Liberator
drive us far from dreams of domination.
May the divine Weaver
make us new hearts of compassion.
May the divine Healer
teach us to cherish our shared frailty.
Amen.

Pausing: Prayer for the day's journey

OPENING

It is time to stop:
to find the point of balance.
It is time to give thanks:
for the seeds we have sown today.
It is time to welcome:
the promise of what will be.

Divine life,
Ground and Glory of our Being,
let us still ourselves within your circle.

ATTENDING

Along the stony path
in the hard city street
your life is expressed.

There is no desert harsh
enough to deny you.
In the lifeless places
you gather creatures and spirits;
you cross the boundaries between earth and heaven.

Under every stone, within every river,
in every flash of wing and scale, fur and swarm,
your life is set free.

May we stop and see
and taste and touch
your creative word.

One or more readings or pieces of music may be heard,
or silence kept.

OFFERING

Christ bears the cross of the world;
we remember those who suffer
and the systems that create suffering.

Christ is the creating Word;
we remember all creatures as icons of glory
and the threat of extinction that hangs over so many.

We remember all those creatures
who spend their love in care and healing,
whose resistance plants hope for justice and peace.
May we be counted among them.

Personal prayers for oneself, others and the world may be offered.

BLESSING

Creating God,
renew us in our walk with you
for the rest of this day's course;
bless our making,
our caring,
our tender courage.
Amen.

Recalling: Prayer for the lengthening shadows

OPENING

We stand at the still point of the day:
a time to reflect.

We move to the threshold of the dark:
a time of gathering.

In the evening hour,
as the sun fades,
may we cherish the stubborn flame of love
burning through the onset of night.

ATTENDING

Free us gently
from misplaced shame,
from denying the gift of who we are.

Free us gently
from envy, bitterness and spite,
from denying the gifts of others.

Free us gently
from masks made to hide our weakness and pain,
from hearts hardened by ill use.

May we see gently,
reading the word and the world
with the open eyes of love.

One or more readings or pieces of music may be heard, followed by a time of silence.

An appropriate canticle may be used (see Appendix).

OFFERING

We gather the fragments of this day:
all that we have known and done and sensed;
all those we have been with in body and in spirit;
all that has made us thankful;
all that longs to be forgiven
and all we need to leave behind.

In the gathering of these gifts
we find you, the One who feeds us.
May you be known to all who hunger.

In the offering of our desire
we find you, the One who enfolds us.
May you be touched by all who dream.

Personal prayers for oneself, others and the world may be offered.

ivine mother, divine father:
to be in you is to be in heaven.
May we hear the wonder that echoes in your name.
May we accept no rule but the rule of love.
May we never tolerate the evil of hunger.
May the hurts we cause be forgiven
and the hurts we receive be healed.
May we remember that we are fragile
and cherish the life we share with all.
For all love, and life and power
is the gift of the Spirit.
Amen.

BLESSING

Bless the dust
from which we are made.
Bless the breath
from which we draw life.
Bless the waters
from which we are born.
Bless the fire
from which we take flame.
May blessings flow
to every quarter of creation
and every moment of time.
Amen.

Letting Go: Prayer for the encompassing dark

OPENING

Under the wings of the Spirit,
the Spirit of the shining dark:
let there be rest.

The flame dies down,
the spring moon rises:
let there be rest.

In the ending of the day,
in the time of letting go:
let there be rest.

ATTENDING

Beyond what can be fixed and named,
in the grace that moves unseen,
open us to encounter your otherness,
in vision, in life, in the face of the other.

In the darkness, a different way of seeing.
In the way of the cross, a different way of living.
In the letting go, a different way of welcoming.

One or more readings or pieces of music may be heard, or silence kept.

OFFERING

In the time of balance,
at the still centre of the crossroads,
we offer to you
worn hands, weary feet, tired minds, bruised hearts;
we offer to you
those who cry in the night
in fear, loneliness, persecution, war and want.

Bind us all, surround us all, lead us through death to life.

Personal prayers for oneself, others and the world may be offered.

**Keep us, holy Spirit of air,
under the shadow of your wings.
Keep us, holy Spirit of earth,
in the darkening of your trees.
Keep us, holy Spirit of water,
in the stillness of your depths.
Keep us, holy Spirit of fire,
in the embers of your heart.**

BLESSING

Stay with us,
in the deep waters of sleep:
healing memory,
nurturing new hope.
Stay with us,
our wounded God,
our undying Love,
our starlit Night.
Amen.

The Fire of Life

Suggested timing: Easter Sunday – Pentecost

Awakening: Prayer for the day's dawning

OPENING

As the fire rises,
as the sun ascends,
may heart and mind become flame,
burning with life's vigour.

As the seed bursts,
as the tomb cracks,
may body and soul become song,
a hymn of praise and glory.

With Christ all things rise:
the cross takes root,
the desert is watered,
the dust of death blossoms into life.

May we be witnesses of this life today:
the life that is not defined by fear and death;
the life that is more than enough for all;
the life that is the glory and song of God through all creation.

ATTENDING

Refresh our insight, living One.
Help us to become children again,
alive to the newness and wonder of things,
ready to ask the troubling questions.

Refresh our compassion, loving One.
Help us to build a world of inclusion
where many voices, bodies and experiences
weave together the web of justice.

Refresh our rage, challenging One.
Help us resist the forces of enslavement and empire,
the colonizing of peoples
and the killing of the earth and its creatures.

Help us to hear you now
in the song of the earth
and the words of its prophets.

One or more readings or pieces of music may be heard, followed by a time of silence.

An appropriate canticle may be used (see Appendix).

OFFERING

Let the victims teach us
the meaning of salvation.

Let the marginalized teach us
the meaning of identity.

Let the earth teach us
the meaning of connection.

Let all those teach us
who uphold their compassion and courage
in the face of hatred
and speak despite all that would silence them.

Personal prayers for oneself, others and the world may be offered.

Divine mother, divine father:
to be in you is to be in heaven.
May we hear the wonder that echoes in your name.
May we accept no rule but the rule of love.
May we never tolerate the evil of hunger.
May the hurts we cause be forgiven
and the hurts we receive be healed.
May we remember that we are fragile
and cherish the life we share with all.
For all love, and life and power
is the gift of the Spirit.
Amen.

BLESSING

Let your blessing, wild and queer,
shake the world;
let thrones of domination fall;
let unheard voices resound.
For yours is the life without limit and fear
and the grave will never more be your home.
You are before us,
the spirit of all the untold stories
still to come.
Amen.

Pausing: Prayer for the day's journey

OPENING

The flame burns steady:
the Spirit is upon us.
We follow the wild tracks:
the Christ is before us.
We let the earth sing:
the Creator is among us.

May the Spirit of the All-Creating Word
fire us with life anew.

ATTENDING

In the greening of the leaves
your life speaks.
As the blossom unfolds,
your love flows out.

Soften our brittle walls
of fear and exclusion.
Quiet the inner voices
of blame and hurt.

May we learn a new song:
a song of creation,
led by the earth;
a song of solidarity,
led by the poor.

One or more readings or pieces of music may be heard, or silence kept.

OFFERING

Enflamer of Hearts,
Unfolder of Scriptures,
Revealer of Hope:
you walk with us
on paths sown with bitterness;
you offer us
the bread and wine of life.

Give us grace
to accept your welcome
and be ready to receive it anew
from the stranger who walks beside us.

Personal prayers for oneself, others and the world may be offered.

BLESSING

Mother of all, Father of all,
our union with you
is delight and creation.
Bless all that inspiration has planted within us
and let our lives be the truth of your love.
Amen.

Recalling: Prayer for the lengthening shadows

OPENING

We stand on the threshold
between day and night:
this gateway, this joining,
this call and answer between the worlds.

We stand on the threshold
between the fire of new life
and the tending of the embers:
this spark, this nurturing,
this promise of hearth and heart.

Move with us, rising Spirit,
through the spaces in between;
retuning our hearts
as we journey by your side.

ATTENDING

Awaken us to the Word within:
the ground of life and love.

Awaken us to the wonder around us:
the weave and weft of grace.

May our knowing be one with yours.
May our loving be one with yours.
May our silence be one with yours.
May our dreaming be one with yours.

And beyond yours and mine,
may all be one
in the giving and receiving
of infinite love.

One or more readings or pieces of music may be heard, followed by a time of silence.

An appropriate canticle may be used (see Appendix).

OFFERING

You are the burning heart of being,
ablaze with love and freedom.

May all we hold in prayer
be held in this never ceasing gift of life.

May we carry that light, that flame, that miracle
into every place of death and despair.

You are the burning heart of being,
ablaze with love and freedom.

Personal prayers for oneself, others and the world may be offered.

Divine mother, divine father:
to be in you is to be in heaven.
May we hear the wonder that echoes in your name.
May we accept no rule but the rule of love.
May we never tolerate the evil of hunger.
May the hurts we cause be forgiven
and the hurts we receive be healed.
May we remember that we are fragile
and cherish the life we share with all.
For all love, and life and power
is the gift of the Spirit.
Amen.

BLESSING

Let the spirit hold
what the fire lit;
let the mind cherish
what the air inspired;
let the body embrace
what the earth nurtured;
let the heart follow
where the water flows.

Let this blessing bind us to you,
who are fire of love, breath of life, body of birth,
the ever-flowing heart.
Amen.

Letting Go: Prayer for the encompassing dark

OPENING

Under the wings of the Spirit,
the Spirit of the shining dark:
let there be rest.

The flame dies down,
the earth holds the embers:
let there be rest.

In the ending of the day,
in the time of letting go:
let there be rest.

ATTENDING

This is the hour of shadow
between the lights of day and dawn.

Open us, in the darkness,
to the ground of truth within us,
the starry sky around us,
the Spirit's presence deeper than words.

One or more readings or pieces of music may be heard, or silence kept.

OFFERING

We offer you this time of silent growth,
praying for healing and rest
for all who are weary and wounded.

We offer you this time of dreaming,
praying for inspiration and renewal
for all whose wells have run dry.

Personal prayers for oneself, others and the world may be offered.

Keep us, holy Spirit of air,
under the shadow of your wings.
Keep us, holy Spirit of earth,
in the darkening of your trees.
Keep us, holy Spirit of water,
in the stillness of your depths.
Keep us, holy Spirit of fire,
in the embers of your heart.

BLESSING

Sing us to stillness
and guide us to peace,
like summer lightning
seen from a far height.
Bless the ending of this day:
all that is complete,
all that is unfinished,
all in you, and you in all.
Amen.

The Greatest Light

Suggested timing: Pentecost – end of July

Awakening: Prayer for the day's dawning

OPENING

The light has gathered
at its fullest flood.
It pours down upon us,
the brightness of grace.

The warmth is rising,
melting ice-bound hearts.
It burns within us,
the flame of passion.

At the midpoint of the year
we ask for the blessings of light:
for vision, for purpose,
for joy in the flowering of creation.

ATTENDING

In your light, we see light:
we seek again the brightness of your glory,
in the face of Jesus Christ.

In your light, we see light:
we feel again the sun giving itself,
gently and generously.

In your light, we see light:
we listen again for the song of joy,
the dance of all creation.

One or more readings or pieces of music may be heard, followed by a time of silence.

An appropriate canticle may be used (see Appendix).

OFFERING

We ask for clarity to choose the wisest path:
the path of liberation and compassion.

We ask for abundance in our hearts:
the strength to end poverty and bitterness.

We ask for passion to speak truth to power:
to claim the dignity of every child under the sun.

We ask for the light that feeds all living things:
to turn our hearts to the healing of the earth.

Personal prayers for oneself, others and the world may be offered.

Divine mother, divine father:
to be in you is to be in heaven.
May we hear the wonder that echoes in your name.
May we accept no rule but the rule of love.
May we never tolerate the evil of hunger.
May the hurts we cause be forgiven
and the hurts we receive be healed.
May we remember that we are fragile
and cherish the life we share with all.
For all love, and life and power
is the gift of the Spirit.
Amen.

BLESSING

May the rising Sun inspire us.
May the inner sun light the way.
At this crowning of the year
may we be blessed,
may we be radiant,
may we be fully alive
in the burning heart of God.
Amen.

Pausing: Prayer for the day's journey

OPENING

You are already here:
in the midst of things;
at the sun's highest point;
under the breathing sky.

Our light from the same source;
our breath from the same spirit.
We are in you
and you in us.

ATTENDING

We pause to notice
the companions we have on this way:
the women and men,
the living creatures,
all differently bodied,
all beautifully imperfect,
all searching, working, rejoicing, suffering.

May the circle of our world and our attention expand.
May we welcome the many faces of truth,
the many bodies that bear your grace.
May the circle of our world and our attention expand.

One or more readings or pieces of music may be heard, or silence kept.

OFFERING

We remember those who work under burdens too heavy to carry:
those who hunger and thirst under a pitiless light;
those burdened with the hateful gaze of others;
and those who are denied the chance to love as they wish.

In you, may we rediscover our common wealth,
our common being:
strong enough to bear difference,
worthy of grace and delight.

Personal prayers for oneself, others and the world may be offered.

BLESSING

May the highest light shine within us,
dispelling the fear from our path.
May the deepest warmth flow from us,
connecting heart to heart.
And may your blessing be to us a circle of flame,
to inspire and protect us through this day.
Amen.

Recalling: Prayer for the lengthening shadows

OPENING

Trees as shadows against the flame;
buildings glow with borrowed light.

We are recalled to a world
shot through with glory,
like blood in the vein,
starlight in diamonds.

We praise the light
and the shadows it creates:
pools of wisdom
distilled from the dusk.

Let the sun not set upon our anger.
Let the light hold our broken blessings.
Let the shadows hold our healing hearts.

ATTENDING

You are the light of the glory of God,
the face of a new creation.
In you, O Christ, the embers of our dreams
are rekindled.

We seek your face.
We seek your word.
We seek your light.

You are in the falling dark,
the roosting call,
the fears and desires
of every creature.

We seek your face.
We seek your word.
We seek your light.

One or more readings or pieces of music may be heard, followed by a time of silence.

An appropriate canticle may be used (see Appendix).

OFFERING

What flows from you
is without measure.
It shatters every label
and passes every border.

In your grace
we will not let violence define us;
we will not let hatred speak for us;
we will not let the past keep our name.

We pray you will be with us
and all wayfarers;
all who yearn to pass beyond
the lines of fear.

Personal prayers for oneself, others and the world may be offered.

Divine mother, divine father:
to be in you is to be in heaven.
May we hear the wonder that echoes in your name.
May we accept no rule but the rule of love.
May we never tolerate the evil of hunger.
May the hurts we cause be forgiven
and the hurts we receive be healed.
May we remember that we are fragile
and cherish the life we share with all.
For all love, and life and power
is the gift of the Spirit.
Amen.

BLESSING

We bless the lingering light;
may it rest upon us.
We bless the night to come;
may it enfold us.
We bless the promise of dawn;
may it lead us.

And may the blessing of the threefold God,
the God of gift and delight and dancing,
compose our spirit
and give us peace.
Amen.

Letting Go: Prayer for the encompassing dark

OPENING

Under the wings of the Spirit,
the Spirit of the shining dark:
let there be rest.

The flame dies down,
the summer moon rises:
let there be rest.

In the ending of the day,
in the time of letting go:
let there be rest.

ATTENDING

In the cooling night
a hidden world awakens.

The owl flies on silent wing;
the fox tastes the beckoning air:
senses sharp, alive in the dark.

**May we hear creation whisper
in us and around us,
beautiful and strange.**

**May our spirit lie open
to the soul of the world.**

*One or more readings or pieces of music may be heard,
or silence kept.*

OFFERING

Give us dreams, living God:
dreams of a planet healed,
in which humanity is just one thread of the weave.

Dreams of peace with justice,
the systems of domination overthrown.

Dreams of a life without why,
shared in common with all.

*Personal prayers for oneself, others and the world may be
offered.*

Keep us, holy Spirit of air,
under the shadow of your wings.
Keep us, holy Spirit of earth,
in the darkening of your trees.
Keep us, holy Spirit of water,
in the stillness of your depths.
Keep us, holy Spirit of fire,
in the embers of your heart.

BLESSING

Under the silent stars
a call sings.
Under the dark horizon
a light flares.
Under the expectant air
a soul breathes.
In the ground of all that is,
in the innermost life,
may we find ourselves blessed.
Amen.

The Gift of First Fruits

Suggested timing: August – early September

Awakening: Prayer for the day's dawning

OPENING

We awaken
to the ripening of the grain.
We awaken
to the rising of the bread.
We awaken
to the abundance of the earth.

For your name, O God,
is fullness of life:
without measure,
flowing over,
more than enough for all.

As your Spirit pulses through creation,
we celebrate our dependence on the earth
and the generosity of your being.
Let this day be one of gathering and giving.

ATTENDING

This is a time of promised gifts:
of seeds grown,
of crops cut,
of sunflowers turning to the light.

In your grace,
let us know what love is coming to birth,
within us and within our world,
and help us to welcome it.

One or more readings or pieces of music may be heard, followed by a time of silence.

An appropriate canticle may be used (see Appendix).

OFFERING

Why gather into barns?
Why hoard the common wealth?
Why enclose the wilds?
Why make beggars of strangers?

You are the gift in the heart of the world:
teach us the law of plenty.

You are the spirit in life's diversity:
teach us the law of plenty.

You are the glory in the face of the stranger:
teach us the law of plenty.

Let us lay down our arms
and find strength in your love.

Personal prayers for oneself, others and the world may be offered.

Divine mother, divine father:
to be in you is to be in heaven.
May we hear the wonder that echoes in your name.
May we accept no rule but the rule of love.
May we never tolerate the evil of hunger.
May the hurts we cause be forgiven
and the hurts we receive be healed.
May we remember that we are fragile
and cherish the life we share with all.
For all love, and life and power
is the gift of the Spirit.
Amen.

BLESSING

A blessing on our gathering:
the harvest of love's seeds.
A blessing on our giving:
born of fearless strength.

A blessing on the first fruits:
the taste of heaven's plenty.
A blessing on the opening road:
the energy to start anew.

This blessing we ask of her:
the Seed of Creation,
the Bread of Life,
the Spirit of the Wild.
Amen.

Pausing: Prayer for the day's journey

OPENING

Within the circle of the day
we gather our hearts.

Within the circle of the year
we rest in the light.

Within the circle of your Spirit
we shine with your love.

In the heart of all life,
in the ground of all being,
in the turning of time:
we are here with you.

ATTENDING

Here, at the moment of readiness,
we listen for the word to be spoken.

Now, at the moment of ripeness,
we hold out our hands for the fruit to fall.

Give us courage:
the strength to hear what is not comfortable;
the vulnerability to learn.

Give us courage:
the strength to act with kindness;
the vulnerability to share the work of peace.

One or more readings or pieces of music may be heard, or silence kept.

OFFERING

The seed once planted
has burst into life.
The path once started
has led to this moment.

We remember what has been gained along the way,
what has been lost.

Holy Life-giver, Holy Light,
we hold within you
the joy of the world,
the pain of the world,
the struggle and the pleasures of all creatures.
May they be complete in you.

Personal prayers for oneself, others and the world may be offered.

BLESSING

May the God who lives in the heart of things
be the source of our life.
May the God who loves in the heart of things
be the source of our compassion.
May the God who is the ground of all things
be the blessing in our midst.
Amen.

Recalling: Prayer for the lengthening shadows

OPENING

The light falls slowly
into the coming dark.

The year turns its face,
still shining,
towards the waning of the light.

What has grown in love,
may it be gathered.

What has bruised our hearts,
may it be tended.

Within the breathing earth,
within the welcoming dark,
within the heart of God,
may we be present.

ATTENDING

Only in the dark
can we find the light.

May we hear the Word.
May it unravel our heart.
May it unsay the labels that define and divide.
May it teach us unknowing.

Only in the dark
can we find the light.

May we taste the Word.
May it be within us.
May it be hidden in secret places only love can find.
May it be the most obvious thing of all.

Only in the dark
can we find the light.

O God, you are black and beautiful,
the one my soul loves. *(Song of Songs)*

One or more readings or pieces of music may be heard, followed by a time of silence.

An appropriate canticle may be used (see Appendix).

OFFERING

A still flame,
shining through the broken world;
a still flame and a sure light.

A shadow heart,
holding all the broken world;
a heart of flesh and longing.

A fragile prayer,
speaking from the broken world;
a prayer of truth and power.

The flame, the heart and the prayer:
we offer these,
bringing the broken world
into the threefold unity
of God.

Personal prayers for oneself, others and the world may be offered.

Divine mother, divine father:
to be in you is to be in heaven.
May we hear the wonder that echoes in your name.
May we accept no rule but the rule of love.
May we never tolerate the evil of hunger.
May the hurts we cause be forgiven
and the hurts we receive be healed.
May we remember that we are fragile
and cherish the life we share with all.
For all love, and life and power
is the gift of the Spirit.
Amen.

BLESSING

Across the threshold of light and dark,
the blessing makes a way.
For all who struggle and suffer,
the blessing makes a way.
With tired limbs and uncertain hearts,
the blessing makes a way.

May this blessing be for all who live,
in the name of the nameless One.
Amen.

Letting Go: Prayer for the encompassing dark

OPENING

Under the wings of the Spirit,
the Spirit of the shining dark:
let there be rest.

The flame dies down,
the summer [*or* autumn] moon is born:
let there be rest.

In the ending of the day,
in the time of letting go:
let there be rest.

ATTENDING

You walk on hidden paths,
the night stars trailing from your skirts.

You speak in strange voices,
the night creatures taking up your song.

You lie on homeless streets,
the night people bearing your image.

Give us dark vision:
a knowing beyond sight
that the world is your body
and all are One.

One or more readings or pieces of music may be heard, or silence kept.

OFFERING

For all creatures
neglected, abused, traumatized and in pain,
we pray.

For all creatures
in poverty, in despair, in confusion and conflict,
we pray.

Teach us to rest in the heart of Christ:
where every vulnerable body belongs;
where every broken heart connects;
where every single life counts.

Personal prayers for oneself, others and the world may be offered.

Keep us, holy Spirit of air,
under the shadow of your wings.
Keep us, holy Spirit of earth,
in the darkening of your trees.
Keep us, holy Spirit of water,
in the stillness of your depths.
Keep us, holy Spirit of fire,
in the embers of your heart.

BLESSING

We are blessed
by the living light.
We are blessed
by the falling night.

We are blessed
in the Word made flesh.
We are blessed
in the Spirit's breath.

We are blessed
by the God inside.
We are blessed
by her arms thrown wide.
Amen.

The Time of Gathering

Suggested timing: Early September – late October

Awakening: Prayer for the day's dawning

OPENING

We stand at the gateway;
the time of balance
between the light and the dark.
We give thanks for the days of summer.

We stand at the point of change;
the turning of the year
from growth to gathering.
We give thanks for the days of harvest.

For the light poured upon us
we thank you, shining One.

For all that has grown within us
we thank you, nurturing One.

For all that will sustain us
we thank you, loving One.

ATTENDING

Jesus spoke
of tiny seeds exploding with life
and fields ripe for harvest;
of the wild growth of weeds
and vines heavy with fruit.

Let the word take root in us.

Let us hear now the word of God
speaking through the earth,
offering life and shelter and food:
more than enough for all.

Let the word take root in us.

One or more readings or pieces of music may be heard, followed by a time of silence.

An appropriate canticle may be used (see Appendix).

OFFERING

Too often we have treated the planet as a commodity,
as raw material to be used and consumed.
We have burnt the skies and sickened the waters.
We have treated our companion creatures with cruelty and indifference.

So we ask for a turning of our hearts.
We offer you the harvest of earth, sea and sky:
may it be the fruit of care and persistent love,
sustaining the richness of living things.

Too often we have treated one another as means to an end:
as things to be labelled, abused and enslaved.
We have not always raised our voices
when our sisters and brothers have been treated with contempt.

So we ask for a turning of our hearts.
We offer you the harvest of our lives:
may it be a gathering of peace and justice,
sharing life in solidarity and courage.

Personal prayers for oneself, others and the world may be offered.

Divine mother, divine father:
to be in you is to be in heaven.
May we hear the wonder that echoes in your name.
May we accept no rule but the rule of love.
May we never tolerate the evil of hunger.
May the hurts we cause be forgiven
and the hurts we receive be healed.
May we remember that we are fragile
and cherish the life we share with all.
For all love, and life and power
is the gift of the Spirit.
Amen.

BLESSING

We praise the firstborn of creation:
in Christ, we and all things are blessed.
We praise the one in whom the fullness of God dwells:
in Christ, life is nurtured and fulfilled.
We praise the one who reconciles all things to God:
in Christ, hostility is healed, everyone belongs.
May the blessing of Christ
fill every creature under heaven.
Amen.

Pausing: Prayer for the day's journey

OPENING

Between the growth and the harvest:
a moment to pause.

Between the outstretched hand and the ripened fruit:
a moment of thanks.

Meet us in our longing, holy Spirit of desire.
Meet us in our gathering, holy Spirit of connection.
Meet us in our sharing, holy Spirit of compassion.

ATTENDING

We remember all that sustains us:
the hidden roots,
the networks of care,
the memories of sun-kissed days,
and shoulders to cry on.

We receive the gift of gathering:
heart drawn to heart,
feeling one another's joy and sorrow,
resisting the lies that fracture our solidarity,
drawing power from the wells of divine strength.

We remember, we receive.
In flesh and in spirit
we are one body.

One or more readings or pieces of music may be heard, or silence kept.

OFFERING

We hold in prayer
those whose harvests have failed;
those who go hungry or disappointed or despairing today;
those whose gathering has been shattered by war or greed.

We are the children of God,
the temples of the Spirit.

We hold in prayer
those who refuse to give up on hope or one another;
those who cherish our uncreated divine life;
those who take a new name
which the world does not know.

We are the children of God,
the temples of the Spirit.

Personal prayers for oneself, others and the world may be offered.

BLESSING

Walk with us,
anonymous God,
unproductive God,
useless God.
Simply be:
with us and in us and through us,
bearing this day on wings of joy.
Amen.

Recalling: Prayer for the lengthening shadows

OPENING

As the day turns,
as the earth breathes,
as the lowering sun stretches shadows into night:
we come under your wing.

You: in every face,
in every whisper of life,
in every touch of compassion,
you are with us.

We bring to you
the memories of hurt and healing,
the doubt and dreaming,
the harvest of the day,
the flesh of our spirit.

You: in every face,
in every whisper of life,
in every touch of compassion,
you are with us.

ATTENDING

Towards evening,
after hard words and dashed hopes,
you showed yourself to the weary and wondering.

Radiant Christ, Son of the Earth,
show yourself to us now.
Speak to our need,
connect our struggles,
give us persistence in our dreams of justice and peace.
Transform the matter of our lives
into the kindling of hope.

For you are the love, human and divine,
that never dies and never runs dry.

One or more readings or pieces of music may be heard, followed by a time of silence.

An appropriate canticle may be used (see Appendix).

OFFERING

Creation is not ours to dominate and define.
It is gift. It is strange. Our names do not confine it.

Creation is the web of which we are strands.
It is many. It is alive. Our hearts are called by it.

Creation is a life more than human.
It is us. It is other. Our lives are bound to it.

We pray that we will be co-creators
with the divine spirit:
learning from nature's creativity,
blessed by all with whom we share it,
held within the mystery of being.

Personal prayers for oneself, others and the world may be offered.

Divine mother, divine father:
to be in you is to be in heaven.
May we hear the wonder that echoes in your name.
May we accept no rule but the rule of love.

May we never tolerate the evil of hunger.
May the hurts we cause be forgiven
and the hurts we receive be healed.
May we remember that we are fragile
and cherish the life we share with all.
For all love, and life and power
is the gift of the Spirit.
Amen.

BLESSING

May we know the blessing of light.
May it fall upon us like rain.
May it shine from the heart's depth.
May it surround us in peace.
May we know the blessing of light.
and carry it into the darkness.
Amen.

Letting Go: Prayer for the encompassing dark

OPENING

Under the wings of the Spirit,
the Spirit of the shining dark:
let there be rest.

The flame dies down,
the autumn moon is born:
let there be rest.

In the ending of the day,
in the time of letting go:
let there be rest.

ATTENDING

Held within the rhythm of creation,
the rising and falling of the spirit's breath:
we listen;
we connect.

Touched by the shadows of the moon,
alive beneath the pale stars:
we listen;
we connect.

We are waiting.
We are expecting.
We are hoping.
We are struggling in the dark
for the first taste of a new world,
for the sharp cry of a new-born God.

One or more readings or pieces of music may be heard,
or silence kept.

OFFERING

We give you the harvest of the day:
what has been learned and lost
and what has marked the pathways of our heart.

We pray for a humbler knowing:
for our hope to come from those who experience poverty and persecution.
May they live and sing aloud.

We pray for a deeper presence:
with all who are struggling in life to find a place,
to shape a voice that is their own.
May they live and sing aloud.

We give you the harvest of the day:
what must be carried and what must be set down
and what must be shared as food for all.

Personal prayers for oneself, others and the world may be offered.

Keep us, holy Spirit of air,
under the shadow of your wings.
Keep us, holy Spirit of earth,
in the darkening of your trees.
Keep us, holy Spirit of water,
in the stillness of your depths.

Keep us, holy Spirit of fire,
in the embers of your heart.

BLESSING

Let us face the dark without fear.
It is the night of creation,
the night of birth.
Let the divine darkness bless us,
and the Christ light guide us,
now and always.
Amen.

The Call of Memory

Suggested timing: Late October – Advent Sunday

Awakening: Prayer for the day's dawning

OPENING

We rise to the dawning of life:
countless beings sing the hymn of creation.
We feel the spirit moving in all things:
the earth, sky and sea bring us healing.
We touch the humming lines of connection:
the web of all things sparkles with energy.

May the Spirit of creation, healing and connection
bless and hold this space, this time, this being-together.
And may all that we bring and all that we are
find a welcome in the silence.

Silence is kept

Through the spaces of city and country,
public and private,

sacred and profane,
neglected and contested,
divided and united,
commercial and communal,
the Spirit makes its exile way:
seeking a home,
seeking a face,
seeking a listening ear.
Spirit of God,
be with us here.

Through the spaces of our lives,
confused and radiant,
hurting and healing,
anxious and confident,
ashamed and proud,
beautiful and broken,
the Spirit walks the inner path:
seeking the truth,
seeking the soul,
seeking the child within.
Spirit of God,
be with us here.

ATTENDING

We watch for the time
when the boundaries between heaven and earth
are wiped away.

We watch for the dawning of the spirit
in the awakening of creation.

We watch for the time
when the presence of God shines out from within us.

We watch for the light of all the living
to meet and bind our hearts in one.

May we be surprised by the mystery of God
always among us:
at the ground of all being,
at the heart of creation,
abundant in poverty,
alive in death.

One or more readings or pieces of music may be heard, followed by a time of silence.

An appropriate canticle may be used (see Appendix).

OFFERING

May we offer uncertainty
to the arrogance of the powerful.
May we offer openness
to the closed doors of hate.
May we offer bridges
across the chasms of exclusion.

May we offer compassion
to the hearts grown cold.

May Christ be our Way,
our Truth and our Life,
who crosses all the barriers
of fear and oppression.

Personal prayers for oneself, others and the world may be offered.

Divine mother, divine father:
to be in you is to be in heaven.
May we hear the wonder that echoes in your name.
May we accept no rule but the rule of love.
May we never tolerate the evil of hunger.
May the hurts we cause be forgiven
and the hurts we receive be healed.
May we remember that we are fragile
and cherish the life we share with all.
For all love, and life and power
is the gift of the Spirit.
Amen.

BLESSING

Faith, hope and love remain:
God has faith in us,

hopes for us,
loves us.
Let us take that good news to all
in what we say and how we live.

And may the blessing of the Spirit of Christ,
the wounded healer,
give fire to our passion, depth to our joy
and tenderness to our love.
Amen.

Pausing: Prayer for the day's journey

OPENING

The speaking of God
is not far away.
It is not in heaven or beyond the sea.
The speaking of God is on our lips
and in our listening heart.

The knowing of God
is not far away.
It is not for those who are wise in their own eyes.
The knowing of God is in our hands
and in our wisdom's heart.

The loving of God
is not far away.
It is not for the pure and the perfect.
The loving of God is in our body
and in our broken heart.

You, our God, are not far away
so that we should have to find you.
You have found us, and known us and loved us
and given us a heart of flesh.

ATTENDING

We walk with a company of witnesses:
the people and moments that have shaped us;
traditions that have oppressed;
traditions that have empowered;
chinks of light that have exposed and inspired us;
voices, gentle and harsh.
The living memory of the past grounds us.
The unresolved pain of the past weighs us down.

Let us be open to them.
Let them speak to us.
Let us meet them
and in that meeting, find healing and hope.

One or more readings or pieces of music may be heard,
or silence kept.

OFFERING

Our prayer: a curling leaf,
a flash of red and gold
in the turning of the year,
the turning of the day.

Nothing stays the same.
From the dying of things
beauty is born,
the magic of life is revealed.

We pray that we might walk with the one
in whom we die, in whom we live again.

Our prayer: a curling leaf,
offered in faith to the one who never stops creating.

Personal prayers for oneself, others and the world may be offered.

BLESSING

May your blessing fall like leaves,
a touch of transformation.
May your blessing be gathered in secret,
ready for the time to grow.

May your blessing be known in life and death
and in letting go of fear.
Amen.

Recalling: Prayer for the lengthening shadows

OPENING

We are on the threshold:
between day and night,
between harvest and winter,
between the frenzy of life and the silence of death.

Meet us here, living and dying God,
she who dances in field and street.
Meet us here, wild Spirit,
he who crosses every border.
Meet us here and light the fire,
let the flame of love burn bright and free.

ATTENDING

Let us hear the shadow voices:
the stirrings of memory,
the traces of those who have touched our lives,
the fragile saints who left kindling for hope.
Let us know, as we are fully known.

Let us sense the Word made flesh:
the one who calls us to remember and rejoice,
the one who shares our humanity to the full,
the one who lives within each moment of compassion.
Let us know, as we are fully known.

Let us hear and taste and touch
the hunger of the flesh for healing and joy,
the laughter of the spirit knowing it is complete,
the 'Yes' of God to all that we are.
Let us know, as we are fully known.

One or more readings or pieces of music may be heard, followed by a time of silence.

An appropriate canticle may be used (see Appendix).

OFFERING

Love made us
and journeys with us,
from the miracle of birth into the mystery of death.

Love becomes flesh
in tears and heartbreak.
Love becomes flesh
in the cry of protest against oppression.

Love becomes flesh
when hunger is fed and dignity restored.
Love becomes flesh
when we delight in creation for its own sake.

May our prayers make a way for love:
a place for love to take shape,
a place to be rooted and grounded
for those who seek justice, peace and the healing of the earth.

Personal prayers for oneself, others and the world may be offered.

Divine mother, divine father:
to be in you is to be in heaven.
May we hear the wonder that echoes in your name.
May we accept no rule but the rule of love.
May we never tolerate the evil of hunger.
May the hurts we cause be forgiven
and the hurts we receive be healed.
May we remember that we are fragile
and cherish the life we share with all.
For all love, and life and power
is the gift of the Spirit.
Amen.

BLESSING

God of gathering,
your blessing is feast and fire,
a place for all in the oncoming night;
your blessing is welcome and wonder,
running to meet us when our hearts sink low;
your blessing is laughter and love,
the gift of a name the world will never know.
God of gathering,
draw us into the circle of your love.
Amen.

Letting Go: Prayer for the encompassing dark

OPENING

Under the wings of the Spirit,
the Spirit of the shining dark:
let there be rest.

The flame dies down,
the autumn moon is born:
let there be rest.

In the ending of the day,
in the time of letting go:
let there be rest.

ATTENDING

In the pause between breathing,
in the falling of the dark,
in the opening of the door:
silence.

In the moment of gathering,
in the coming of night,
in the presence of the stars:
welcome.

Nameless God,
God of many names;
silent God,
God of the life-giving Word;
let us be in you,
in the mystery of you.

One or more readings or pieces of music may be heard, or silence kept.

OFFERING

We pray for all who stand on the edge:
between one journey and another;
between life and death;
between joining and parting.

Guide our ways, Christ our Light,
so we can walk without fear
and lend a hand to those who stumble.

Personal prayers for oneself, others and the world may be offered.

Keep us, holy Spirit of air,
under the shadow of your wings.
Keep us, holy Spirit of earth,
in the darkening of your trees.
Keep us, holy Spirit of water,
in the stillness of your depths.
Keep us, holy Spirit of fire,
in the embers of your heart.

BLESSING

A blessing on our gifts
and on our sharing.
A blessing on our past
and on our growing.

A blessing on our rest
and on our roaming.

May the God of birth,
the Word of compassion,
the Spirit of freedom
encompass us and all creation,
this night and always.
Amen.

PART TWO

Praying with the Elements

Preface

As explained in the Introduction, these four rites are intended as a complement to the seasonal cycle found in Part One. By focusing on the symbolic associations of the traditional four elements of air, fire, water and earth, they offer an opportunity to engage with particular spiritual qualities and imagery. One rite is offered for each element, which can be used at any appropriate time of day. Brief suggestions of accompanying symbolic actions are made, but you are invited to let your imagination put flesh on these bones!

Praying with Air

To focus on new life, new possibility, clear thinking, freedom of spirit, inspiration, Spring, dawn and birth/childhood.

OPENING

We shall rise up like eagles,
riding on the shimmering air.

We shall go as the wind goes,
searching where it will.

We are open to the dawn,
to the moment of new birth.

We are drawn to the breath,
to the time of inspiration.

Give us, Holy Spirit,
a clear mind,
an open heart,
a first step
into your future.

ATTENDING

Speak to us a Word of clarity:
a breath to loosen tired thoughts.

Speak to us a Word of freedom:
a storm to shake the bonds of injustice.

Speak to us a Word of invitation:
a still centre where all are welcome.

**Within the weaving of the Spirit,
within the touch of air on skin,
within the atmosphere of love,
speak to us a Word of grace.**

One or more readings or pieces of music may be heard, or silence kept.

A symbolic action may be performed, such as quietly focusing on the breath, or lighting incense.

A SONG OF THE SPIRIT

Inspired by John 3
The wind blows where it chooses,
and we do not see its end.

In the night of unknowing,
we must learn to begin again.

Those who look for signs and wonders
must find themselves reborn.

In the darkness of God's womb,
we see truth for the first time.

Beyond the world of condemnation
and the stigmas of oppression,

God turns the world upside down,
a gift to reveal what we love.

We are known for who we are,
lifted to the light of truth.

In the breath of the spirit of Christ
there is a nameless freedom.

Free of purpose and control,
we live for life itself.

For the wind blows where it chooses,
the Spirit of a wild God.

Glory to the God in the lifting air.
Glory to the God in the heat of the sun.
Glory to the God in the water's flow.
Glory to the God in the darkness of earth.
Glory to God in all creation.

OFFERING

We scatter these seeds on the wild wind,
these offerings of life and hope.
We let them go where the Spirit will,
a gift of faith and trust.

May the forces of enslavement,
which kill thought and deaden hope,
be uprooted by the Spirit,
who cannot be contained.

Personal prayers for oneself, others and the world may be offered, especially for the cleansing of the air and all who suffer from its pollution and global climate change; and for freedom of thought and inspiration.

Divine mother, divine father:
to be in you is to be in heaven.
May we hear the wonder that echoes in your name.
May we accept no rule but the rule of love.
May we never tolerate the evil of hunger.
May the hurts we cause be forgiven
and the hurts we receive be healed.
May we remember that we are fragile
and cherish the life we share with all.
For all love, and life and power
is the gift of the Spirit.
Amen.

BLESSING

Blessed be to us the untamed air.
Blessed be to us the learning mind.
Blessed be to us the Spirit of freedom.
Blessed be to us the open sky.
May the blessing of the living God
give us wings to fly.
Amen.

Praying with Fire

To focus on passion, creativity, power, fertility, confidence, Summer, noon and adolescence/adulthood.

OPENING

The inner light unfolds,
a kindling of the spirit;
and we are ablaze with you,
God of Fire and Life.

In the heat of your jealous love
your heart claims us,
claims all of us:
body and soul, heart and mind.

You come to awaken us:
a river of light,
running through our veins,
consuming fear and failing.

Fall on us, burning God!
Deepen our passion for you.
Make us all flame,
all flame.

ATTENDING

In the glow of the Spirit's light,
in the presence of the undying flame,
we gather to hear the stories come alive again.

As Moses stood before the burning bush,
and heard the mystery of your nameless name,
we gather to unlearn what we think we know.

As women and men received the gift of the Spirit,
freeing voices long divided,
we gather to share what is common to all.

One or more readings or pieces of music may be heard, or silence kept.

A symbolic action may be performed, such as lighting a candle or small fire.

A SONG OF FIRE

Inspired by Acts 2
This is fire: a speaking in tongues
crossing the borders of nation and language.

This is fire: a sharing in common,
uprooting the structures of racism and wealth.

This is fire: a passion for new life,
for communities of honesty and justice.

This is fire: a spirit poured out
on all our different human bodies.

This is fire: the visions of the young,
the ardent dreaming of the old.

This is fire: slavery overthrown,
and every child of God a prophet.

This is fire: fullness of life
and the pleasure of God in our flesh.

**Glory to the God in the lifting air.
Glory to the God in the heat of the sun.
Glory to the God in the water's flow.
Glory to the God in the darkness of earth.
Glory to God in all creation.**

OFFERING

**Jesus said, 'I come to throw fire on the earth.
I wish I had found it burning.'**

Your words are fire to us,
to take us through the wasted places of our life
and make them rise again from the ashes.

Your Spirit speaks with tongues of flame,
undoing the language of domination,
opening hands to share in common.

May we follow the pillar of fire
away from the place of slavery.
May our restless heart lose its fear,
fierce in our love for liberation.

Jesus said, 'I come to throw fire on the earth.
I wish I had found it burning.'

Personal prayers for oneself, others and the world may be offered, especially for the fullness of life and the creativity of passion to flourish for all creatures.

Divine mother, divine father:
to be in you is to be in heaven.
May we hear the wonder that echoes in your name.
May we accept no rule but the rule of love.
May we never tolerate the evil of hunger.
May the hurts we cause be forgiven
and the hurts we receive be healed.
May we remember that we are fragile
and cherish the life we share with all.
For all love, and life and power
is the gift of the Spirit.
Amen.

BLESSING

Our God, you have not made us
to cower in fear and self-doubt;
you have made us to be fully alive,
strong and brave in the centre of your heart.
May your blessing fan into flame
what you have shared with our soul.
Amen.

Praying with Water

To focus on depth of wisdom, emotions, intuitions, dreams, Autumn, evening and maturity.

OPENING

We swim in the ocean of the Spirit,
held within her limitless love.

Grace falls upon us, a gentle rain,
released from the heart of God.

We touch the depths and the air-kissed waves,
the flow of feelings, connecting all to all.

We open mind and heart, body and spirit
to the living water,
to the flowing love,
to the God around us and within us.

As the deer longs for flowing waters,
so my soul thirsts for you, Holy One.

ATTENDING

May deep speak to deep.

The water that gives birth to all creation
also gives birth to us.

The water that lives in every creature
also lives in us.

The water that refreshes the dry places of the earth
also renews us.

May deep speak to deep;
and may we hear the murmur of the Spirit,
the wisdom of water,
deeper than words can say.

One or more readings or pieces of music may be heard, followed by a time of silence.

A symbolic action may be performed, such as drinking water or washing one's face or feet.

A SONG OF THE RIVER

Inspired by Ezekiel 47
The river flows from the Sanctuary,
a blessing for the land and its creatures.

It washes away bitterness and satisfies thirst,
a living stream from the heart of God.

It is the grace of healing,
and the promise of food for all.

In the depths of God's love,
we are immersed, we are sustained.

It is a life without conditions,
beyond all we can measure.

Wherever the river flows,
everything will live.

It will teem with living creatures
and feed the growing trees.

See and taste that God is good,
in the waters of creation.

Glory to the God in the lifting air.
Glory to the God in the heat of the sun.
Glory to the God in the water's flow.
Glory to the God in the darkness of earth.
Glory to God in all creation.

OFFERING

We long for transformation,
your compassion for all who thirst.

Water changed into wine:
creation received as miracle and delight.

Deserts blossoming and bursting into song:
wilderness received as spirit and freedom.

The tree of life, planted by the river:
the cross received as healing and hope.

We long for transformation,
your compassion for all who thirst.

Personal prayers for oneself, others and the world may be offered, especially for a deepening of our intuition, people's access to fresh water and for the cleansing of our rivers and oceans.

**Divine mother, divine father:
to be in you is to be in heaven.
May we hear the wonder that echoes in your name.
May we accept no rule but the rule of love.
May we never tolerate the evil of hunger.
May the hurts we cause be forgiven
and the hurts we receive be healed.
May we remember that we are fragile
and cherish the life we share with all.
For all love, and life and power
is the gift of the Spirit.
Amen.**

BLESSING

The living water restore us;
the fathomless depths renew us;
the falling rain awaken us.
May the blessings of water be ours to share,
running free and clear,
and glinting like diamonds
in the light of glory.
Amen.

Praying with Earth

To focus on stability, rootedness, embodiment, patience, persistence, Winter, night and death.

OPENING

You: in the roots of the mountain.
You: in the dark of the earth.

You are our rock, the ground of all we are;
in you we stand and none shall move us.

You are the core, the hidden deep;
in you we are planted and connected to all.

God of the living soil and the ancient stone:
in you we are known beyond all memory.

We praise you for the vibrancy of matter,
for the deep time of the earth.
We praise you for the body that we are,
for the sensuous web of life.
We praise you for the time of dying,
and the glory of the night.

ATTENDING

Let the earth speak its name
like water flowing from the rock.

Let the earth speak of growth,
its roots hidden in darkness.

Let the earth speak of beauty,
of evolution's wonder.

Let the earth speak of harmony,
of making space for all.

Let the earth speak of difference,
of worlds that do not belong to us.

And let the earth be silent
when our grasping words fall short.

One or more readings or pieces of music may be heard, followed by a time of silence.

A symbolic action may be performed, such as putting one's hands in soil, or feeling the weight and texture of a stone.

A SONG OF THE EARTH

Inspired by Song of Songs 2

He comes upon the mountain paths,
like a deer leaping for joy.

She comes on ways unknown,
powerful with her love.

As the flowers rise from the earth
and the blossom drops from the branches,

so love speaks to love
as the soul flies to God.

Love is sweetness and support,
a resting place for head and heart.

Love is passion and delight,
the voice of the singing Spirit.

In the cleft of the rock,
in the hidden place of the earth,

the mystery of love is born,
the fullness of love bears fruit.

Let us see your face,
let us hear your voice.

Let us run on the yielding earth,
until the day breathes its last.

Glory to the God in the lifting air.
Glory to the God in the heat of the sun.
Glory to the God in the water's flow.
Glory to the God in the darkness of earth.
Glory to God in all creation.

OFFERING

Christ is the Son of the Earth;
may he teach us to cherish it.

Where it is turned into raw materials,
let us respect its inner worth.

Where its living creatures are driven to extinction,
let us renew its diversity.

Where injustice denies people a place upon it,
let us overcome the systems of exclusion.

Christ is the Son of the Earth,
his cross planted into the soil
as a protest against empires,
invasions and colonies.
Let us follow in the way of his rebellion,
in the paths of the living earth.

Personal prayers for oneself, others and the world may be offered, especially for a sense of stability, for the just distribution of land, the preservation of habitats, and all affected by soil degradation and erosion.

Divine mother, divine father:
to be in you is to be in heaven.
May we hear the wonder that echoes in your name.
May we accept no rule but the rule of love.
May we never tolerate the evil of hunger.
May the hurts we cause be forgiven
and the hurts we receive be healed.
May we remember that we are fragile
and cherish the life we share with all.
For all love, and life and power
is the gift of the Spirit.
Amen.

BLESSING

After Genesis 49.25
The blessings of the heavens above,
the blessings of the deep beneath,
the blessings of the body of birth,
the blessings of our forebears,
the blessings of the ground of all:
support us, give us strength
and make us fruitful in loving.
Amen.

Appendix: Canticles

These canticles are for optional use with the patterns for daily prayer, especially with the rites for Awakening and Recalling as part of the 'Attending' section (possibly before or following a reading).

According to my suggested presentation below, there are three canticles that can be used at any time of year, and two for each of the eight seasons.

The canticles are all loosely based on biblical material. I emphasize 'loosely', because I am certainly not pretending that these are translations or even paraphrases of the source material. Rather, I have taken inspiration from the texts and from specific aspects of their imagery, but these are compositions that make no claim to translate or represent the original. This has also allowed me to draw on material that would not usually fit into the shape of a canticle.

The first three canticles take as their starting point the Magnificat, Benedictus and Nunc Dimittis (all from Luke 1 and 2), which are much used in morning and evening prayer across a number of church traditions. The two canticles for each season are inspired respectively by Hebrew Bible (or Greek Apocrypha) and New Testament texts.

I have not attempted to include any psalms, since complete inclusive versions of these exist and may be used to supplement the present volume by those who would prefer this way of praying Scripture. These include *The Inclusive Psalms* (AltaMira, 1997) and *The Grail Psalms: Inclusive Language Version* (Collins, new edition, 2004).

Canticles and psalms offer ways of saying and sharing prayers that allow us to *inhabit* the imagery of Scripture. There are various ways of doing this, and I leave it to local custom and exploration to settle on the most fitting one. If used individually, they can be read slowly, in silence or aloud, pausing between each line or couplet. Groups may arrange them so the leader and the rest of the congregation say alternate couplets; or a group could simply be divided into two roughly equal halves to create a similar effect of call and response.

If desired, each canticle can end with a praise formula (a 'doxology'), such as:

Glory to the One from whom all life flows.
Glory to the Word who touches the heart.
Glory to the Spirit who goes where she will.
Glory to you, the Beginning and the End.

For any season

A MAGNIFICAT

My soul bears witness to love without measure
And the joy of God takes root within me

I am known and named by the blessed One
In my poverty and care, God is born

God's strength is made perfect in weakness
A rumour of love echoes through the ages

The powers of the world are hollow
Our systems of injustice and scorn fall to dust

The voice of the silenced is heard
And salvation comes from the persecuted

There is no more hunger in God's reign
There is more than enough for all

The craving of the rich leaves them empty
A hunger that consumes itself

God is the pulse in the vein of creation
In the soul of every living thing

In the story of my forebears
In the laughter of Sarah and Abraham's faith

In the journey from slavery
And the heart-songs of the prophets

My soul bears witness to love without measure
And the joy of God takes root within me.

A CREATION BENEDICTUS

Blessed be the One who creates
Who delights in the rhythm of life

From the strangeness of matter
A universe is spun

Within the heart of being
Life emerges, vibrant and searching

Through the intricate paths of evolution
It becomes complex and beautiful

Blessed be the One who creates
Who speaks through the bodies of all creatures

On the fearful clarity of the mountain top
The Spirit sings of transformation

In the unknown deeps of the ocean
The Spirit sings of rebirth

In wood and river, field and desert
The Spirit sings a new song

May the wonder of creation open us
To a life beyond our understanding

Blessed be the One who creates
Who travels across the threshold

With reverence for all creatures
Let us make peace with the sky

With reverence for all lands
Let us make peace with the earth

With reverence for all becoming
Let us make peace with the sea

May our senses be filled with the play of creation
With a wisdom of the living heart

Blessed be the One who creates
In whom all things are One!

A SONG OF PARTING

May we travel onward in peace
Letting go of all that does not serve love

May we walk to the edge of light
Led by faith into the unknown

May we open our spirit to mystery
To the glory that shines around us

May we share the dreaming of God
And wake to the newness of creation.

The Path of Shadows

A SONG OF THE WILD SPIRIT

Inspired by Job 38
Come with me, says the Spirit of Creation
Come to the deep places of the earth

Come to the moment when the sea is born
And the waters teem with life

Join with me in the song of the stars
Of the morning stars shouting for joy

For I am she who gives the morning
I am the living Spirit of the dawn

I shake the foundations of the arrogant
And those who set themselves up as gods

Those who decide who is worthy and who is not
Those who deny my gifts are for all

I am found in the fields of light
And the places of deepest shadow

I fall in the rain and flow with the river
I am the father and mother of it all

I am the wisdom that lives in Orion
And binds itself to the human heart

I am wild and undefined
No story tells my beginning and end

I am wild and undefined
And you are the child of my heart.

A SONG OF THE GIVER

Inspired by various parts of the Letter of James
Every perfect gift, every act of compassion
Comes from the unwavering source of love

In the heart of shadow lies One who gives light
An unchanging gift of presence

This gift is given to all
By the word of truth we are given birth

Let us transform this word into living
Let us speak and act with kindness

Every spark of being, every new creation
Comes from the undying source of life

This life is shared with all
For all creatures breathe the Spirit

It is care for those in weakness
And compassion for those who are broken

Let us bring this faith to life
In mercy, patience and peace.

The Growing Light

A SONG OF DAWN

Inspired by Isaiah 9
Our steps have crossed the darkness
And now we see your light

On the quiet earth, under the leafless trees
We glimpse the coming growth

You take our small faith, our human weakness
And multiply our joy and confidence

For the word of life is born in our world
A word to break the power of oppression

A word that stops the march of war
A word that speaks from the child's heart

It is a word that will never be silenced
A joy that will be made complete

For we are your children
And the word is born within us.

A SONG OF GLORY

Inspired by 2 Corinthians 4
This body of earth is mine
Changing and fragile

I have heard them say
Leave your body, it stands in the way

It is not perfect, it is not complete
Its desires are impure, it will betray you

But I know my body is a gift
Dust shaped by the loving hands of God

I know that God is no stranger to the earth
To the body, to dirt and desires

I will not be the body they want
I will not be a pale reflection of their ideal

For the glory of God shines in every atom of my being
The broken body of Jesus gives strength to mine

So I will not lose heart
My beating heart of flesh

I will not give up hope
The hope of my desires

For the light of glory
Is shining now within me

Spilling over, beyond all measure
It touches the edge of creation

It is the knowledge of God
Carried in the glory of the flesh.

A SONG OF NEW LIFE

Inspired by Isaiah 35

The earth has found its voice
It sings with the growing of all things

The dry and dead places
Will thrill with life again

Breaking the surface of our despair
Shaking the roots of our indifference

Love unfurls a riot of colour and life
And leaves no room for fear.

Be strong: you are known to me
Your own name is on my heart

You will sense the coming of your God
In the beauty of creation

The water of life will free your tongue
And you will share in the dance of the deer

You will never be lost to me
You will find a way to my welcoming heart.

A SONG OF THE SEED

Inspired by Mark 4
The teaching is a seed
A new world beginning to open

Settling into the deep earth
Ready to break through, an uprising of life

In darkness and mystery, the seed is sown
Giving birth to the dissident rule of God

The presence of God is known as it grows,
Wild and unmeasured, it changes everything

The borders that keep out those who do not belong
Are overgrown with beautiful weeds

The overflowing presence of God
Is the measure of our life-giving love

God is the sower of the seed
Our hearts the field that lets it grow

Thanks be to the Living One
Who shares with us the delight of creation.

Heart of Spring
Summer
Equinox
(July)

A SONG OF LOVE'S DELIGHT

Inspired by the Song of Songs
I call the winds to awaken
For the fragrance of the earth to rise

I am open to my beloved
Who loves without power or pretence

We eat and drink: honey, wine and milk
We are drunk with love

We share in the ecstasy of creation
And no one can judge us

The one who loves is glorious as night
bright as the sun dawning on the earth

They say our bodies are not perfect
But we are beautiful as we are

Every part of us sings of love
Every fold and wrinkle is truth

Deeper than words, freer than air
Love listens and accepts

For love is a burning fire
A passage from death to life.

Love - burning fire
Life to death

A SONG OF COMPANIONSHIP

Inspired by Luke 24

You come near to us
In the coldness of despair

You are our companion
In the greyness of doubt and fear

You call us and know us
And share your inner heart

Like your mother Wisdom
You teach us what is precious

More precious than hoards of wealth
Is the story of your love

And in the falling light
You make a place for us

You break the bread and bless the wine
And we know you as you are

Our hearts are burning within us
As you speak to us here and now.

The Greatest Light

A SONG OF JUBILEE

Inspired by Leviticus 25
Let the trumpet sing out its call
Let the years of debt be done

When oneness is restored
The chains of submission have no place

Let the earth be given rest
Let creation breathe in peace

Free from domination
May all have life in fullness

In communities of compassion
May no one be left out

May weakness receive respect
And all have food enough

May work be valued with justice
And no one count as worthless

May the year of jubilee rise like the sun
And slavery melt away as the dew

We remember those before us
Whose law was one of freedom

We walk in the path they trod
Loving the God of liberation.

A SONG OF LIGHT

Inspired by John 9

The sun gives its light freely
It lives as it passes away

It does not judge, it does not cling to life
It is the fountain of our being

The light of the world shines freely
It gives life to all who receive it

It does not judge by human standards
It is not of this world, with its powers and prisons

It respects no limits on its grace
It makes the slave free and calls the nameless one its child

The light of the world gives no glory to itself
It creates no kingdom of its own

The greatest light needs no papers
No guarantee of its power

It is known in its self-giving
And the truth that sets us free.

The Gift of First Fruits

A SONG OF THE LAW OF LOVE

Inspired by themes from Leviticus 23 and Deuteronomy 10, 11, 30 and 31

The harvest is upon us
The first fruits of a world renewed

The land belongs to God
A common gift to all

Offer it to the Spirit of Creation
Share it with the poor and excluded

Let no fence enclose it
No wall create misery

Let us go unshod in the ways of the Creator
On the holy ground of creation

Let hearts be fierce in love for the stranger
Let God be our praise in the work of compassion

We bind ourselves to the law of love
We make it the centre of our wisdom

A wisdom to hand to our children
A wisdom to nurture the dying

It is not far off in heaven
It has not wandered across the sea

It is not locked in a vault
Or hidden behind barbed wire

It sings in our voices
And beats in our hearts

In belonging or in exile
It is the presence of God

In every moment of every day
We hear it say: 'Choose life!'

A SONG OF THE FIRST BORN

Inspired by Colossians 1
First born of creation
In you the roots of all things are entwined

First born of creation
Before you, all the world's powers are empty

First born of the children of God
From your heart, the fullness of God overflows

First born of the children of God
You are found wherever justice takes root
and compassion grows

First born of the new creation
We are called to make peace with the earth

First born of the new creation
We are called to make peace with our mortality

First born in all things
Take our hostile anger and resentment

Take our fear and greed
And make us one flesh, one body in you.

The Time of Gathering

A SONG OF THE HEART

Inspired by Jeremiah 31
In the wilderness, in the waste places of our lives
We have found your presence

When you seemed far from us
You found us with an everlasting love

You build us up
When we come crashing down

You gather every different body
That bears the labels of shame and scars of suffering

And bring us to a place of healing
A radical place of acceptance

You empower us to live with joy
Confident in your boundless love

We do not need to hide our tears
For all we are is known to you

This is the new covenant, your promise
Which you gave to your people Israel

A love beyond the height of heaven
A love deeper than the earth's foundation

A sharing of the heart and spirit
A knowing deeper than words can tell.

A SONG OF RESURRECTION

Inspired by Romans 6

Into the depths of loss Christ falls
Into the death of hope

He takes nothing with him
But changes everything

He takes us there
Through fear and failure

To the life that is without cause
Except the love of God

The narrow self
With its terrors and targets

No longer defines
Who we are to become

Dead to the world
Of submission and indifference

We live with Christ
In the very heart of God

No longer slaves to purpose
We live without a why

Our laughter rises up
To every cruel dominion

Shaking it to the core
With resurrection joy.

A SONG OF WISDOM'S WEALTH

Inspired by Wisdom 7

I descend from the first-formed child of earth
A mortal, breathing the common air

Without nurture I could not have lived
Now I tread the suffering earth

Honours and titles turn to dust
Riches rust away to nothing

Words like scars define the world
Who can live and who must die

We are told which body we should attain
Which soul we should have been

But wisdom cannot be named and caged
Her wealth cannot be counted

In her hands is life, freely given,
A treasure that never fails

In her is friendship with God
In her, creation comes alive

Wisdom is one, but has many faces
No creature is strange to her

She is the living breath of God
The consciousness divine

In her, we do not need to prove ourselves
For we are already loved

She is the bridge from death to life
Our memory and hope.

A SONG OF FAITH IN THINGS UNSEEN

Inspired by Hebrews 11–12

Not every vision can be seen
Not every truth can be spoken

Faith travels in the darkness of trust
To places still unknown

It makes us strangers to the world
The world of fearful certainty

Faith does not stay in its place
It will not let things lie

Faith opens a place for creation
It offers a gift without price

Faith lives in the voices and stories
Of the people who have shaped us

In the daring of Ruth and Abraham
In the courage of Rahab and Esther

In the shining face of Moses
And the music of David

In Hannah and Mary
And their songs of revolution

In the prophets and dreamers
Who gave life to God's word

In all the ancestors who have given us life
Whose memory is carried within us

Those who touched the world with kindness
Those forgotten and ignored

In faith they are with us
Unseen, they are our companions

They are the cloud of witnesses
With us, they are invited to the feast

Let us set down the weight of despair
And the tyranny of common sense

Taking the way of the cross
Letting go of anxious clinging

We live the joy of Christ in faith
The promise of a world restored.